I Can Do It!

I Can Swim

By Meg Gaertner

level 1
little blue readers

www.littlebluehousebooks.com

Little Blue House is distributed by North Star Editions:
sales@northstareditions.com | 888-417-0195

Produced for Little Blue House by Red Line Editorial.

Photographs ©: Shutterstock Images cover, 7, 11 (top), 11 (bottom), 12–13, 15 (top), 15 (bottom), 16–17, 19, 20–21, 24 (top left), 24 (bottom left), 24 (bottom right); iStockphoto, 4, 8–9, 22–23, 24 (top right)

Library of Congress Control Number: 2022901675

ISBN
978-1-64619-580-0 (hardcover)
978-1-64619-607-4 (paperback)
978-1-64619-660-9 (ebook pdf)
978-1-64619-634-0 (hosted ebook)

Printed in the United States of America
Mankato, MN
082022

About the Author

Meg Gaertner enjoys reading, writing, dancing, and being outside. She lives in Minnesota.

Table of Contents

teacher
class

I Can Swim

I take a swimming class.

I learn from a teacher.

The teacher holds me up.
I feel the water
around me.

teacher

I swim safely.

I swim only if an adult is around.

adult

I wear goggles.
They protect my eyes.
I wear floaties.
They keep me
above water.

goggles

floaties

I lie on my back.

The water holds me up.

I'm floating!

floating

I kick my legs underwater.

I paddle my arms.

I stay in one place.

underwater

I reach one arm forward.
I pull it through the water.
Then I use my other arm.
I'm swimming!

arm

I swim across the pool.

I reach the side.

I have a big smile.

I know how to leave

the water.

I find a ladder.

I climb up.

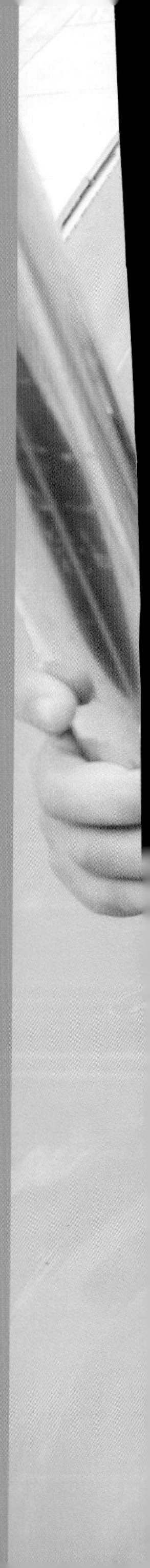

ladder

I walk to the diving board.

I jump into the water.

I make a big splash!

diving board
splash

Glossary

floaties

splash

goggles

underwater

Index